T0381216

THE POWER OF

3

LESSONS IN LEADERSHIP

STEVEN MAYS

AuthorHouse™
1663 Liberty Drive
Bloomington, IN 47403
www.authorhouse.com
Phone: 1 (800) 839-8640

Published by AuthorHouse 02/12/2016

ISBN: 978-1-5049-6522-4 (sc)
ISBN: 978-1-5049-6524-8 (hc)
ISBN: 978-1-5049-6523-1 (e)

Library of Congress Control Number: 2015920617

Print information available on the last page.

Any people depicted in stock imagery provided by Thinkstock are models,
and such images are being used for illustrative purposes only.
Certain stock imagery © Thinkstock.

This book is printed on acid-free paper.

Because of the dynamic nature of the Internet, any web addresses or links contained in this book may have changed
since publication and may no longer be valid. The views expressed in this work are solely those of the author and do not
necessarily reflect the views of the publisher, and the publisher hereby disclaims any responsibility for them.

The Navy provided for the symbols
(Brigade of Midshipmen flag, Class of 1974 crest, and gold submariner's dolphins)

"Endorsement by the United States Department of the Navy is not intended nor implied."

Acknowledgements

To my wife, Saint Barbara, and my wonderful children, Patricia Jeanne, Katie, Steven, Ryan, Jessica, and Brooks who make my life worthwhile. To my classmates from the United States Naval Academy class of 1974 who prove the old saying that the best ships in the world are friendships, especially Tate, O'Neill, Eustace, Phelps, and Dunn who provided unvarnished review and critique of this work along with Reverend Mark Boyea. And last, but certainly not least, to my USS Los Angeles shipmates who tolerated me through my leadership growing pains. I had a lot to learn and they were willing to teach me, especially my Chiefs; Maes, Bowers, Fritz, Davis, Ford, and Tillman. I thank you all.

Foreword

"You should write a book." Several friends and acquaintances of mine have dropped that line on me and each time I laughed at them. I laughed because I had no idea how to write a book. Also I found it hard to believe that anyone would publish it given that I don't have a PhD behind my name or some other claim to fame. I just like to tell stories. Not just stories for the sake of telling stories, but stories that make people laugh or more importantly make people think. Or as Arsenio Hall would say while resting his finger on his temple, "Makes you go hmmmm."

I had something less than a sheltered childhood. I grew up with Southern roots where story telling is a means of day-to-day communication. Talking to someone without a story to go with it was like a peanut butter sandwich without the peanut butter. Don't get me wrong, I like bread a lot, but I like peanut butter sandwiches even more. As an Air Force brat, I also grew up in a lot of different places; West Virginia, Virginia, Florida, Texas, South Carolina, France, West Virginia, Virginia, Texas, Libya, Spain, and Texas.

That was just getting from birth through high school. I attended twelve different schools along the way (some more than once) and met people from different walks of life, different countries, and different religions. (And by different religions, I don't just mean Christian, Jewish, or Islamic. I witnessed monster differences in religions from my neighbors even though they were all Christians, but that is another story for another time.) So far, I have probably proven that I am, was, and always will be a motor-mouth. Like they say down home, "He jus' cain't hep it."

After high school, my path turned to Annapolis, Maryland and the United States Naval Academy. I wanted to serve and be part of that line of service academy graduates that have given so much to this country. I wasn't aiming to be famous, I just wanted to do something to serve because I had seen so many other places and people that were not free and I wanted to preserve that blessing for others. OK, that may sound corny, but it isn't.

Following commissioning as a brand new ensign and getting my first salute from my father (how cool is that?), I set off to become a submariner. After Nuclear Power School, Nuclear Power Prototype Training, and Submarine School, I finally reported aboard the USS Los Angeles (SSN-688) pre-commissioning crew in Newport News, Virginia. There we oversaw the construction of the first of the new class of fast attack submarines, conducted initial sea trials, and conducted fleet operations in the Atlantic, Mediterranean,

Pacific, and Indian Oceans. It was an incredible learning experience, not just about nuclear power and submarines, but about people and leadership. And I had a lot to learn - just ask the people who used to work for me. I had a lot to learn.

After my tour in the Navy, I worked in several different organizations involved with conducting risk evaluations of nuclear power plant operations. I worked at National Laboratories, private consulting firms, and the Nuclear Regulatory Commission. I was exposed to the culture, style, and techniques of "management" and "leadership" in those environments and evaluated the similarities and differences between military, civilian, and government expressions of these. I was also exposed to formal and informal training on leadership as I rose through the ranks of various organizations.

Then one day I got an email from a classmate asking if I would be willing to act as a facilitator for the Capstone Seminar for seniors at my alma mater. The Capstone Seminar is a daylong leadership forum for first class midshipmen culminating their formal leadership training before they graduate and head to the fleet as commissioned officers in the Navy or Marine Corps. The service academies don't have freshmen, sophomores, juniors, and seniors. Navy has plebes, youngsters, 2nd classmen, and firsties. And while the Naval Academy had a Math department, an English department, a Chemistry department, and other academic departments, they surprisingly had no formal Leadership Department during my time there. If it surprises you, just imagine how it surprised me at the time. When I went to be a facilitator at my first Capstone Seminar, I was instantly amazed at how the Academy had changed to embrace Leadership as a formal discipline through the Stockdale Center for Ethical Leadership headed by retired Marine Colonel

Arthur Athens. As my class was sponsoring the seminar, I reconnected with classmates and they all said the same thing, "Where was this when we were here?" We were all impressed by the quality of the Mids (that's Navy-speak for a Midshipmen, not a Middie, please!) and their formal training in leadership.

This was the catalyst that caused me to consider writing about the principles I discovered through the college of hard knocks that could (and should) have been taught to me when I was younger. As I said earlier, I do not have a PhD so I am not an academic expert with a curriculum vitae full of published papers. Nor am I a retired admiral, the CEO of a Fortune 500 company, a movie star, or a well-known politician. Which raises the question, "Why should anyone listen to what I have to say about leadership?"

Good question. And my answer may surprise you. I am a failure and so are you! Not one of us is perfect or even close. We all fall short and have to pick ourselves up and move forward. It is the process that is taught in some schools these days as "experiential education." We used to call it hard knocks, getting your feet wet, or trial and error. At any rate, with each failure, we have the opportunity to learn and improve or to stagnate in place. I was never comfortable with stagnation; it bores me. Plus I have a little bit of Don Quixote in me that makes me want to make a difference for others so they don't have to fail as often as I did in order to succeed.

> "And the world will be better for this.
> That one man scorned and covered with scars,
> Still strove with his last ounce of courage,
> To reach the unreachable star."

So, with my experiential base; with some formal training such as the Federal Executive Institute; with personal education through reading about leadership; with many failures and subsequent successes; and with a penchant for story-telling, I humbly offer, for your consideration, some thoughts on leadership with the hope that they may support you on your path of service and be of benefit on your journey "to run where the brave dare not go."

Table of Contents

Acknowledgements...iii

Foreword... v

Three is Everywhere 1

Foundational Principles..6

Dealing with Missed Expectations 22

Dealing with Conflict 26

Probability Theory..33

Leadership Versus Authority...38

What Is The Opposite Of Love? 41

What Do Leaders Do? 44

What Is Leadership?...47

About The Author 51

Three is Everywhere

What is your favorite number? Ask that question of a group of people and you will get a range of different answers. They are as varied as the individuals asked. My favorite number is three. I found over time that three keeps coming up in too many places for it merely to be a coincidence. Being a math major and practicing probabilistic risk assessment for many years taught me to be skeptical of coincidences. Let me give you a quirky example.

My late father's birthday was December 9th. My first son was born on December 9th. My late father-in-law's birthday was December 9th. Two people in a family with the same birthday is not all that rare. But, three is just a bit much. (There is a classic mathematical rationale why any group of 30 or more people is likely to have two people with the same birthday, but I digress.) My wife and I joke that God was trying to tell us something but we were two thick-headed to listen. When my wife came out of the bathroom holding the EPT test strip in her hand that showed she was pregnant, we were overjoyed. Then came the doctor visit for the ultrasound and not one, not two, but three babies present. Oh boy! We walked around in shock for a few days trying to figure out how we were going to handle having triplets and finally decided it was a Nike moment – Just Do It. So, on 11/11/1996 she gave birth to three wonderful children at the Franklin Square Hospital in Baltimore, Maryland.

But that wasn't the end of the eeriness. As it turns out, no one carries triplets to term these days; it is too risky. So doctors perform Caesarian Section births about a month early for safety's sake. That's right, if they had been carried to full term, they would have been born on December 9th. Now if you are humming the theme song from "The Twilight Zone" right about now, you're correct. But it gets weirder.

Franklin Square Hospital had experienced a triplet birth a few years earlier. And one of the two doctors performing our delivery was also there for the birth of that previous set of triplets. But, instead of standing by the operating table during delivery, she was on the table giving birth to triplets.

You just can't make this stuff up. So, the number three had a big impact on my psyche. The more I looked around the more I saw the number three. Here are a few examples.

1. Ever try to sit on a one-legged stool? OK, if you're a member of Cirque du Soleil you can probably do a one-armed hand stand on a one-legged stool and contort your body into unimaginable positions while beautiful music plays amid a laser light show; but most of us in the real world can't do that.
2. We live in a three-dimensional world. I have a height, width, and unfortunately more "depth" than I care to admit.
3. Christians believe in a Triune God (Father, Son, and Holy Spirit).
4. The mission statement of the U. S. Naval Academy (which we all had to memorize on our first day there) is *"To develop Midshipmen morally, mentally, and physically and to imbue them with the highest ideals of duty, honor, and loyalty in order to graduate leaders who are dedicated to a career of naval service and have potential for future development in mind and character to assume the highest responsibilities of command, citizenship, and government "* Notice the three sets of threes: morally, mentally, and physically; along with duty, honor, and loyalty; and command, citizenship and government.
5. Three way communication – command, echo, acknowledgment.
6. Comedy (Larry, Curly, and Moe – the Three Stooges).
7. Baseball – Three strikes and you're out; three outs per at bat.
8. Really old baseball – Tinker to Evers to Chance.
9. Music – Three Coins in a Fountain, Three Dog Night.
10. Movies – The Three Faces of Eve, The Three Amigos.

The list could go on for quite a while but you get the gist. An interesting story about one of the entries above. Some baseball historians believe that the Chicago Cubs of the early 1900s were the best team in all of baseball history. In fact, it was in 1908 that the Cubs last won a World Series title. They had an amazing double play combination during those years of shortstop Tinker, second baseman Evers, and first baseman Chance. They became famous not just for their fielding exploits, but because the Cubs were from the "Second City" of America and they kept beating the beloved Giants of New York (the undisputed

First City of America). The New York sportswriters were so upset that one penned a poem that ended up cementing their legacy.

Baseball's Sad Lexicon

These are the saddest of possible words:
"Tinker to Evers to Chance."
Trio of bear cubs, and fleeter than birds,
Tinker and Evers and Chance.
Ruthlessly pricking our gonfalon bubble,
Making a Giant hit into a double –
Words that are heavy with nothing but trouble:
"Tinker to Evers to Chance."

Leadership Lesson – Mission vs. Personality

Now you are probably wondering what this has to do with leadership, so an explanation is in order. Tinker's and Evers' feelings for one another went way beyond dislike. They despised one another. They even came to blows on the field in 1905. Nowadays, we have all seen the replays on ESPN where a fight breaks out at a ball game and both benches empty and the bullpen players rush in from the outfield, etc. Imagine the poor guys on the other team witnessing this fight. "Hey look, a fight, let's go!" cries one voice from the bench. As people begin to exit the bench a voice answers, "Wait a minute, that's Tinker and Evers fighting." "Well what are we supposed to do now?" Cue the music for "Ripley's Believe It or Not"!

If you know much about baseball, you probably know that turning the double play is one of the riskier events in a game wherein your health is totally dependent on the good will of the person trying to "break up the double play" and the person trying to provide the ball to the "turner" so they can complete the play without the need of an orthopedic surgeon. In the early days of baseball when people like Ty Cobb were notorious for coming into second base with "spikes up" (and in Cobb's case, sometimes sharpened), getting the ball there just a bit late or in the wrong spot could end a player's career. So the fact that these two players who hated each other's guts were willing to do what was necessary to win despite their personal feelings says a lot about their dedication to their team and the game.

They feuded for years and would not speak to one another except as necessary in the course of a game. Only 33 years later when both were asked to appear on a radio broadcast (where neither one knew the other was invited) did they talk to one another. This is an extreme example that it is not necessary to like everyone you work with in order to be successful. (I warned you I was a story teller.)

4

One principle I learned long ago is the KISS theory. "Keep It Simple, Stupid." Along a similar line, Einstein is attributed with saying "Everything should be made as simple as possible, but no simpler." when developing theories to explain the physical world. So with that in mind, and the discussion above, it should be easy to understand my fascination with the number three.

Accordingly, what follows are constructs of a leadership philosophy where the number three figures prominently. This is in no way meant to imply that three is the only number of use in leadership. However, in trying to keep things as simple as possible, but no simpler, and with apologies to Covey's "Seven Habits of Highly Effective People", John Wooden's "Pyramid of Success" (with 15 blocks and another 12 principles), Kiersey's four personality types, etc, I hope you will find these constructs to be useful in your leadership journey.

"The Power of Three" Leadership Construct involves three main areas. These are:

1. **Foundational Principles** - The bedrock of leadership activities that form the basis for all actions
2. **Dealing with Missed Expectations** – The keys to understanding how missed expectations occur and how to address them
3. **Dealing with Conflict** – The process of coping with and handling situations that challenge your core principles and ethics

Each of these areas will also involve three main ideas (surprise, surprise). Enjoy!

Foundational Principles

Bedrock. Foundation. Cornerstone.

These are three words one often hears in the building trades, but they are also important in leadership. In this context, they mean the unwavering, ever-present, and ever-lasting principles that form the core of a leadership ethos. And like civil engineering or architecture they build upon one another.

There is a principle in mathematics (I was a math major, so it shouldn't surprise you I use math analogies) regarding the number of independent variables necessary to define a position within a construct. These are called coordinates and there are a minimum number of coordinates necessary to describe with complete certainty and no ambiguity a particular location within the construct. In mathematics there is also a phrase used to determine the truth of an argument. The phrase is "necessary and sufficient". Necessary meaning that without the condition, the end result cannot be achieved and sufficient meaning that once reached, no additional conditions are needed.

So, let's examine a common mathematical construct, the Cartesian plane. It is named after Rene Descartes who was a French mathematician, philosopher, and lawyer (his father insisted on this training though he rarely employed it). He was the philosopher famous for the statement, "Cogito, ergo sum" (I think, therefore, I am.). Back to math, in a two-dimensional space, one needs exactly two coordinates to define any point on a plane. (In a three-dimensional space, three are needed.)

Therefore, if you wish to designate a point in a Cartesian plane, you would typically use an "x" and a "y" coordinate to designate its location from the origin. Thus, the point (1, 1) on the Cartesian plane is located one unit along the direction of the x-axis from the origin and one unit in the direction of the y-axis. They are the necessary and sufficient information needed to locate the point in the plane. But are they the ONLY coordinates for that point?

NO! A point can be described by any orthogonal set of two coordinates. For example, the polar coordinate system can also be used to reach the point (1, 1). Polar coordinates use a magnitude (length) and an angle to define the same point. The point (1, 1) in polar coordinates is ($\sqrt{2}$, 45°). One starts at the origin and moves $\sqrt{2}$ distance along an angle from the x-axis of 45° and arrives at the same point. One can remember the Pythagorean Theorem for the magnitude and basic trigonometry for the angle if desired. In fact, engineers will tell you that the ability to convert between the two is very important in any calculation involving vector addition (Cartesian) or multiplication (polar).

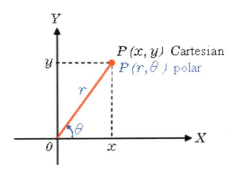

The point is there is more than one set of coordinates that are foundational for the Cartesian plane that are both possible and useful. I am not so foolish or so arrogant that I will lay claim that my three foundational principles for leadership are the only three that exist or are the only three that are most important. Retired Colonel Arthur Athens speaks of the three C's: Competence, Courage, and Compassion. And quite frankly I have an affinity for his approach. My foundational principles are somewhat similar, not unlike Cartesian coordinates and polar coordinates which can be derived from one another. So, without further ado, my Foundational Principles for Leadership:

HONESTY

COURAGE

TALENT

Of course, you need to know what I mean by each of these terms so you can evaluate your individual situations.

HONESTY is the ability to see the world and your situation within that world AS IT IS!

> Not as you would want it to be.
> Not as you think it should be.
> Not as it could be if those dummies in charge would see things your way.

There is a term in modern lexicon for this way of thinking, "Keepin' it real, yo!" And perhaps using the term honesty instead of realism is more dramatic, but you hopefully get the point.

Honesty, in this context is not about preventing lying, cheating, or stealing. You can find that set of triplets in honor codes at various institutions and it is an honorable pursuit. In his book, "The Road Less Traveled", Scott Peck wrote about everyone having a map of the world that one is constantly updating as new experiences and situations arise that impact life. In this context, honesty, is about having the best map possible based on your experiences and striving to understand and update that map realistically as you move forward. You need to know where you are and where you came from to better determine where to go next and how to get there. Otherwise you end up in the world of "The Adventures of Buckaroo Banzai Across the 8th Dimension" where, "No matter where you go, there you are." Or in other modern parlance, "If you don't know where you are going, any road will get you there."

This definition presents many difficult issues. First, those with less experience and less reflection on that experience will be at a disadvantage because their maps may be critically incomplete when faced with a tough situation. Second, those with more experience may likely have a more accurate map, but can come to believe that their map is the only correct one and that those with less experience cannot possibly have a valid map. In any case, it is likely that any two people will have maps with some commonality as well as some differences. The key here is not to decide whose map is "right" but to determine which map is most appropriate for the situation and get as many people as plausible to operate from the same map. Having a common moral compass and a common map from which to navigate is a key test of leadership and one of the most difficult efforts leaders must undertake. But it is important that everyone in an organization have some common elements to their maps so that the direction they are heading is better understood and easier to achieve. Below is a comical example of how being on different maps can impact an organization. I have no idea how to properly attribute this passage other than to quote the great comedian Milton Berle, who was once reputed to have said, "I never heard a joke I couldn't steal."

HOW STUFF HAPPENS

In the beginning was the plan.
And then came the assumptions.
And the assumptions were without form.
And the plan was without substance.
And darkness was upon the face of the workers.
And they spoke among themselves saying,
"It is a crock of bull and it stinketh."
And the workers went unto their supervisors and said,
 "It is a pile of dung and none may abide the odor thereof."
And the supervisor went unto their managers and said,
"It is a container of excrement and it is very strong, such that none may abide by it."
And the managers went unto their directors, saying,
"It is a vessel of fertilizer, and none may abide its strength."
And the directors spoke among themselves, saying to one another,
"It contains that which aids plant growth and it is very strong."
And the directors went unto the vice presidents, saying unto them,
"It promotes growth and is very powerful."
And the vice presidents went unto the president, saying unto him,
"The new plan will promote the growth and vigor of the company, with powerful effects."
And the president looked upon the plan and saw that it was good.
And the plan became policy.

Hopefully you can see that there were maps with some similarities at each step but without enough commonality to carry through the underlying message. At each level, the map changes somewhat until at the conclusion it bears no semblance to the original situation. So, eventually the opposite of what was intended came to pass. One contributing factor in this type of incident is the process of packaging (spinning) a story to please the boss out of fear of making the boss upset. In his 14 principles for improving business efficiency, Deming's eighth principle was "Drive out fear, so that everyone can work effectively." This is equally true in leadership because a valid map is difficult to produce when fear is injected into the process. This type of problem (different maps and different spin) also feeds into "The Abilene Paradox" made famous by Professor Jerry Harvey of The George Washington University who discusses how false agreement is the more common (and disastrous) feature of some organizations rather than turmoil brought about by internal disagreements.

COURAGE consists of three things (surprise, surprise, surprise). COURAGE is the ability to overcome fear to take action for the benefit of others without regard to the risks to yourself.

It may seem odd to mention fear in the definition of courage, but it is essential. Without some fear, taking action to benefit others is an act of charity not courage. Similarly, if there is no risk to yourself, then the action requires no courage. All three are needed to define courage just like an x and y coordinate is sufficient to find a particular point on the Cartesian plane. Below are three points that come out of acts of courage.

1. There is an acronym, INAM, which fits here. It's Not About Me. It's about someone else. In leadership parlance, this could be anything from a person to person action or an action leading to the success or failure of a mission for a large group of people. In any case, selflessness is an attribute you will often find attributed to leaders. The old Army saying is, "Officers eat last."

2. Courage is about actions to benefit others. Self-interest and self-esteem are important individually, but leadership involves sacrifice for the benefit of others.

3. Lastly, compassion is not a weakness, it is a strength. A leader MUST care about how actions affect individuals in order to have the slightest chance to lead them in any endeavor that could impact their well-being.

The last of the three foundational principles is TALENT. TALENT is the ability to take effective action to deal with problems/situations for the betterment of the individuals and the organization. Notice that there is an "AND" in that sentence rather than an "OR". Leaders always strive to benefit the individuals AND the organization. It may not always be possible to do so, but it should be the goal of every leader.

As before, there are three attributes that constitute TALENT; knowledge, skill, and perseverance.

1. Knowledge is required in order to be effective. Anyone can order someone else to perform a task. All that requires is authority over them. Knowledge is needed in order to know what to do, how to do it, who can do it, when to do it, what resources are needed to do it and what the potential impacts of doing the task (or not doing it) may be. You can't ask a third grader who hasn't even delved into long division to conduct an analysis using calculus. Without knowledge the task is doomed (or at least extremely unlikely to be successful).

2. Skill is needed to actually perform the tasks at hand. I know how to hit a golf ball. I do it often. In fact, I end up hitting the ball so often that I would starve if I tried to make my living on the PGA tour. To perform that task (play on the PGA level), I would need much more skill so I could hit the ball less often in each round of golf. Similarly, the leader and the people under his/her command need skills in the tasks before them to have a chance of succeeding. Staff members may be treated as equal and interchangeable parts of an organization for accounting purposes, but they are made up of individuals with differing skills. A leader should know what those skills are and allocate tasks accordingly. In basketball, there is a saying, "Don't ask your point guard to dunk and don't ask your center to dribble the ball up the floor." Sure, there are point guards who can and do dunk, but none who really make their living doing that alone. And there are some centers who can dribble competently. But the successful coach puts each in a position to maximize their skills for the betterment of the team.

3. Perseverance is required in order to hone the knowledge and skill above into a reliable, repeatable, and dependable capability. How do you get to Carnegie Hall? Practice, practice, practice. Honing

the skill is an essential part of improving one's talent. There are many people who can throw a baseball 100 miles per hour. Not many can throw it to a specific location with accuracy. Those that can are in the Hall of Fame. Those that cannot, well, who knows where they end up. Remember that Michael Jordan was cut from his high school varsity basketball team. Perseverance is what made his talent so amazing.

Human beings are a discriminating bunch by nature. We are able to see, hear, smell, taste, and feel a myriad of things. Combined with our brains, we are able to sort these variations into categories of similar and dissimilar natures. So, it is one of our natural tendencies when given any number of things to try to put them in some order from first to last or best to worst. Having said that, I intend to shock you somewhat.

Leadership Lesson – Role of Talent

Of the three foundational principles just delineated, TALENT IS THE LEAST IMPORTANT.

That may sound a bit strange, so I want you to think back over your lifetime of achievements and failures. See how many times your biggest failures in life were due primarily to a lack of talent. I'll wait a few seconds for you to resurrect those memories you were hoping to forget. Take your time, it will be worth it in the end.

OK, time's up!

I have done this exercise many times. In fact, I do it often. And I have yet to come up with a single case of a major failure in my professional or private life where I failed due to a lack of talent. Now it may be different for you individually, and I have no hard experimental data to prove this in an academic sense, but when I have presented this challenge to numerous people whom I know and respect as leaders, I have yet to hear of a case where lack of talent was the primary problem.

Looking back a few years in recent history, let me give a few examples. To be fair, I will pick on both Republicans and Democrats as well as the military. Does anyone think that Richard Nixon was impeached by the House of Representatives and resigned the Presidency before the Senate could try him for the Watergate cover-up because he lacked talent? Sticking with presidents, does anyone think that Bill Clinton lost his law license for lying to a court in a deposition because he lacked talent? And in the more recent past, probably one our finest generals since Eisenhower, General David Petraeus ended up resigning as CIA director when it was revealed he had an affair with a woman writing a book about him. Was that a lack of talent? Catch my drift?

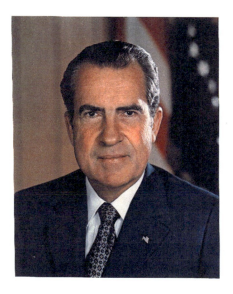  

One more thing about talent. If you send a Little League baseball player to take your place at the plate in the World Series in bottom of the ninth with two outs and the bases loaded needing a hit to avoid losing the series, his inability to get a hit off of a major league pitcher is likely do to a lack of talent. However, you sending him up there is not. It is either a lack of honesty in not realizing he is not competent for that task or a lack of courage by sending him up there in the first place.

Please do not think I imply that talent is UN-important. It is critical to sustained success. You must improve your skills continuously to enable your growth and provide experience and training for those following you in whatever career path you choose. In fact, if you look at any organization's performance review process, you will likely see many more items relating to talent than to leadership in that process. My point here is simply that more catastrophic failures in leadership occur in areas other than talent. Now for some less dramatic examples, but illustrative nonetheless. This time I will start with myself.

Leadership Lesson – Honesty in Action

The military has many traditions and each branch and service specialty has its own. One that is consistent is the old saw, "Rank has its privileges." This one manifests itself in an interesting way in the Navy. When a ship is at sea, someone has to drive it. That person is the Officer of the Deck (OOD) who is responsible for the safe navigation of the ship as well as discharging whatever mission duties are at hand. The portion of the crew fulfilling these duties are called watch standers, or simply the watch. So, if there has to be watch standers, there has to be a schedule and this is called the watch bill. Normally, the most senior officer standing the OOD watch makes out the watch bill. Being most senior, he selects the watches he will stand first, then goes to the next senior OOD to select his watches, and so forth until the most junior OOD gets whatever watches are left over.

During my last deployment, I was second only to the senior watch officer (SWO) but noticed that he never came to me to select the watches I would be standing. In fact, I always ended up standing the "mid watch" which on a submarine is the six hour period between midnight and six in the morning (0000 to 0600 to those familiar with military time). Beside the fact that this was the time most people slept (but I couldn't) the mid watch was also responsible for cleaning up whatever messes were left behind by the day watches and catching up on whatever jobs no one else found time to do during the day. So, beside the difficulty of getting sleep during the day when so much training, drills, and routine paperwork and interactions were occurring, it was also the watch that got a lot of extra burdens others had put off. Needless to say that wasn't making me terribly happy.

So I went to the SWO and asked him why the junior officers were getting better watches than I and why I was never consulted about watch assignments as was my due based on seniority. What happened next was a real eye-opener for me. The SWO was dutifully up to his ears in paperwork when I asked him these questions in a less than genteel manner. But he was busy, so without even looking up he said, "That's what the Captain wants." Not to be deterred, I demanded to know how I had made the Captain mad enough to do this to me. This time, the SWO stopped his work, laid down his pen, sighed deeply, and gave me that LOOK. You know, the steely-eyed stare you give your children when they just don't seem to get it. At the end of his sigh, he said, "Because you dummy, that's when he sleeps!" (It was actually a bit saltier than that, but you get the picture.)

You could have knocked me over with a feather, if you could find me because I had just mentally crawled into a hole and pulled it over my head. It hit me like a ton of bricks. My commanding officer (CO) didn't want any other officer as OOD while he slept other than me because he trusted me and relied on me to do the job well.

Why didn't I think of it that way? Because I wasn't being HONEST about my situation. My map was messed up. And even when my SWO tried to break it to me gently, I was so invested in MY version of MY map that I failed to update it with the new information. So, he had to shock me a bit to wake me up. Now, besides being humiliated at myself, I recognized that my CO was actually placing confidence in me and I felt better about having the mid watch. My pride was taken down a few notches, but I learned a valuable lesson that day about updating my map and seeing the situation AS IT IS, not like I thought it should be or how I wanted it to be.

There is another leadership lesson here that may be a bit subtle. Have you noticed it yet? If you said, "Why didn't Steven know the reason for being given the mid watch all the time?" go to the head of the class. If my CO wanted me on the mid watch, why didn't I know that?

Another point to ponder is that when a situation initially appears to be wrong, it may be useful to look for a positive reason rather than assuming a negative one before challenging the circumstances.

Everyone who has ever house-broken a dog knows how this works. As the owner, you know that a puppy has a small bladder and stomach and that they sleep a lot. So, every time they wake up or eat, there is a natural urge to relieve themselves. The more successful trainer also knows that dogs like to be rewarded by their owners. So, the good trainer takes the dog out right after waking and waits for nature to take its course. And when it does, the trainer goes "gaga" over the puppy and maybe even gives it a treat. Pretty soon, the puppy learns to like being treated that way and will do almost anything to wait until out in the yard to relieve itself. So, why would a leader treat his dog better than his staff? Beats me, but I never knew why I was getting the mid watch assignments.

Leadership Lesson – Courage and Compassion in Action

The next story involves my daughter of whom I am extremely proud, so bear with me as I brag on her. My daughter is one of the most empathetic people I have ever known. She can tell when others are feeling down before they even notice themselves. At the start of first grade she was coming home each day having not taken even a nibble out of her lunch. When queried about why she wasn't eating lunch, she indicated that there wasn't enough time. So, naturally, my wife and I contacted her teacher and asked why she didn't give her enough time to eat. When she said she had plenty of time, we asked her to check on her the next day at lunch. She told us the story of why she wasn't eating and my heart fell out. It still makes me emotional to this day.

It turns out there was a boy in her class whose family was lucky enough that his mother didn't have to work outside of the home. In fact, this young boy had spent almost every waking moment of his life interacting with his mother. She was the first face he saw in the morning, the face he saw all day long, and the last face he saw before he fell asleep each night. When he got to school and there were kids to interact with and a teacher to fulfill the adult role in his life he was fine. But at lunch time the kids were sent to the lunch room, sat down, and had their lunches brought to them to eat. They were told to be quiet, stay in their places and eat their lunches. All the support he had earlier vanished and his separation anxiety would overwhelm him causing him to cry. So, my daughter would go sit with him and talk to him during the entire lunch period so he wouldn't feel bad. In doing so she would neglect her own lunch. It was all I could do to stay composed when she came home from school that day. I let her know how proud I was of her helping a classmate in need while also letting her know she could still eat while doing so. Sometime it's amazing what a child can teach you if you just pay attention.

Speaking of COURAGE, I want to share with you a story that I heard from Professor Jerry Harvey while attending the Federal Executive Institute (FEI). As I noted earlier, Professor Harvey is known for his work on The Abilene Paradox. I won't belabor that story here except to say that Professor Harvey discusses how organizations reach "agreement" when they don't really mean it and how that can have dire consequences. He tells the story of a time at FEI when he did his Abilene Paradox presentation and a member of the class came up to him and pulled a folded piece of paper from his wallet. He showed it to Professor Harvey and then told him what it was. Turns out, it was a list of reasons why a space shuttle launch should be postponed to a later date. This mission was already behind schedule and another delay would be hurtful for both budgetary and public relations reasons. At a meeting with senior staff, a manager at NASA went around the room requiring each person provide a GO or NO GO recommendation. With everyone recommending GO and the fact that the items on the list for NO GO were not definitive, a GO recommendation was made. That mission was the last launch of the space shuttle Challenger and that man had carried that reminder with him ever since. How would you like to be carrying around a piece of paper like that in your wallet?

Having the courage to say no to the boss is a difficult thing to do. Leaders need to encourage people to be up front with their misgivings about a task. Sometimes the remedy is a simple matter to resolve. Other times not so much. But an environment where agreement is treasured above the truth is guaranteed to fail catastrophically at some point in time. You need look no further than the story of the emperor's new clothes to see examples of fear preventing courage from taking action. In fact, the fables and fairy tales of yore are an astonishingly good source of leadership lessons. (The boy who cried wolf, the ant and the grasshopper, the emperor's new clothes, Chicken Little and the sky is falling, etc.)

So I recommend to you that in every leadership situation you encounter you invoke HONESTY, then COURAGE and then TALENT.

Foundational Principles

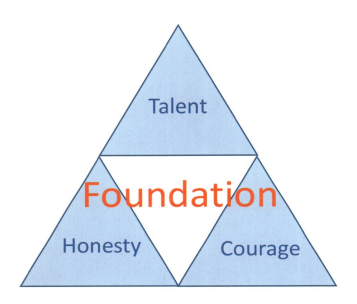

Dealing with Missed Expectations

General Eisenhower once said, "I have always found that plans are useless but planning is indispensable." Years before, Moltke said "No campaign plan survives first contact with the enemy." And Murphy's Law states, "If it can happen, it will happen."

All of the above lead to one inevitable conclusion: every leader in every position will have to deal with a situation where expectations are missed. Naturally, these can span the range of truly innocuous to catastrophic and leaders who can't tell the difference and respond accordingly will suffer the consequences of such short sightedness. So, what is a leader to do when expectations are missed? Keep in mind throughout this discussion that the premise is that the expectation is realistic, relevant, and attainable. As noted in the previous chapter, asking the Little League player to hit a major league fast ball in the World Series is not a realistic, relevant, or attainable task for the coach of a team to employ. So, we will start our discussion of dealing with missed expectations with that assumption in place.

An expectation is missed. Why? In order to correct a problem it is necessary to understand why it occurred. Otherwise, how would you know whether your actions will have any impact on the problem in the first place? Not surprisingly, there are three main attributes of missed expectations each with three factors. The three attributes of a missed expectation are:

1. **The person(s) didn't know what to do.**
2. **The person(s) didn't know how to do the task.**
3. **The person(s) didn't want to do the task.**

To make things simple for non-rocket scientists such as myself, I refer to this threesome as **what, how, and wanna.** When a problem occurs involving these three items, leaders are on the hook for 1 and 2. The staff is on the hook for 3.

In order to carry out a task, a person(s) needs to know what needs to be done. It sounds so simple, but it is surprising how often this one is missed. A sweeping generality is not a definition of what to do. I want people to look good when the client comes in for a meeting. OK, I know you want to impress the client, but what does that mean? In Michael Crichton's book "Rising Sun" there are many of examples how what seems to be appropriate in American law enforcement interactions with American firms that is different for Japanese firms interacting with Japanese law enforcement. In fact, one of the most interesting examples is his comparison between American and Japanese problem solving. "In America, we fix the blame, in Japan we fix the problem."

A leader must ensure that "what" is communicated to those who will complete the tasks. I will violate my use of the number three here and say that leaders need to communicate, communicate, and communicate with their staff. And when they think they have done enough, communicate even more. It is never too late to make sure everyone is on the same page with "what". That is, operating with the same map.

Probably more often, expectations are missed because someone doesn't know "how" to do the task at hand. As a leader, if you give someone a task and you do not know whether they know how to do it, YOU are the problem. The biggest issue in this arena is the word assume.

You probably know the old joke, "assume" makes an "ass" out of "u" and "me". Still, it is usually a foregone conclusion that a person(s) being assigned a task knows how to do it. While convenient, this is primarily laziness on the part of the leader. A conscious action to ascertain whether those receiving the tasks truly know what it takes to do the task should be an integral part of every leader's decision making process when handing out assignments.

While I noted earlier that the leader is on the hook for items 1 and 2, in reality, the staff is also on the hook for item 2. In the event the staff do not know how to do a task or are not sure how to do it, it is important for them to ask how the task is to be performed. The staff have a responsibility to know how to do the task or at least know where to go to find out how to do the task before accepting responsibility for doing so.

OK, so now the person knows what to do, knows how to do it, but still doesn't complete the task as expected. If they were given sufficient time and resources to accomplish the task, there is only one factor remaining – wanna – and that one is on the person assigned to do the task. Unfortunately, it is human nature to jump directly to item 3 to look for the reason that an expectation is missed. Normal, intuitive, and wrong. Why didn't so and so do what they were supposed to do? Can't they do anything right? How hard is it to do this simple task? ETC. ETC. ETC. We've all been there, but the true measure of a leader in such a situation is to first think whether the leader did enough to rule out items 1 and 2 from the situation. Only then, should the focus turn to the individual's willingness to perform the task.

This leads to the inevitable discussion of motivation. Some people like to think that good leaders "motivate" their team/staff. There are a number of academic studies about positive, negative, and neutral "motivations". Maslow's hierarchy of needs discusses how needs at various levels of existence influence a person's behavior. All of this is true, but there is a mistake in believing that the leader is in control of an individual's motivation. While a leader may have authority and power to influence the surroundings in which a person operates, the motivation to accept, reject, or change that surrounding lies with the individual. In that manner, the leader does not actually "motivate" people so much as the leader tries to match the individual's natural motivations to accomplish the tasks at hand. The leader facilitates the individual's motivation.

I have never experienced a team member who got up in the morning thinking, "I'm going to be a worthless slacker today because that is what I am naturally motivated to do." That doesn't mean I haven't experienced some worthless slacking from time to time. However, my experience is that the causes of slacking off such as depression, despair, and low self-esteem have more to do with the occurrence of slacking off than any "motivation" that leaders attempt. Most people want to be successful in their lives and most have things they prefer to do. So, leaders who can recognize those internal motivations and influence environments so that the individual's motivation matches the needs of the organization are the ones who are most successful.

No one likes to admit failure. In an organization where authority and power are vested in individuals concomitant with their position in the organization the problem is magnified. There is an inherent bias that the individual with the vested power answers only to those with higher authority. Yet the discovery of problems within an organization are almost always apparent first to individuals of lesser power and authority. Along with power and authority comes a natural assumption that those vested with it are more likely to be correct when assessing and dealing with problems. Why else would they be put in those positions?

Therefore, the burden of proof falls upon the individual with less power and authority to convince the more powerful individual that they are responsible for taking action to resolve the problem. Remembering the earlier reference to the emperor's new clothes, this puts the subordinate in a delicate situation and can complicate the process of effective communication so that the problem can be expeditiously addressed. Further, if an organization acts in a manner that treats "accountability" as a six syllable synonym for "blame", the problems are further magnified. This is why it so important for a leader to accept the fact that it is the leader (not the follower) that is primarily responsible for the first two root causes of the occurrence of an unmet expectation. Without a clear understanding of that principle and the humility to admit imperfection, the dynamic becomes one where only when a follower's actions are demonstrably perfect can the actions of a senior be challenged. This condition is poison to an effective organization and leaders must strive to eradicate it whenever it occurs.

Dealing With Missed Expectations

Dealing with Conflict

Once again we need to start with a definition. In this discussion, conflict is a difference between what is expected of a person and their core values and principles (ethics and morals). In this sense, it is an opposition that involves an emotional response driven by the difference between what is demanded from an individual and what is acceptable to that individual. So, in this sense it is like missed expectations discussed earlier but on a much larger and more profound scale.

So, what to do when presented with a conflict? Lt. Calley, "Waste that village (My Lai)." "Load those Jews on the train for Auschwitz." From the Lehman Brothers collapse, "'I need to report an extra $20 million.' The analysts are not expecting results to be $20 million less than they should be so to make it OK, I'm just stealing from the future temporarily. I'll make it up next quarter. And so on and so on." From afar, it seems surreal that there really are people who do terrible things despite knowing that they are wrong at the time. Yet it happens. So, what do you do as a leader when confronted with a serious conflict?

"Bodies on Trail" © 1968 by Mr. Ronald Haeberle, Used with permission.

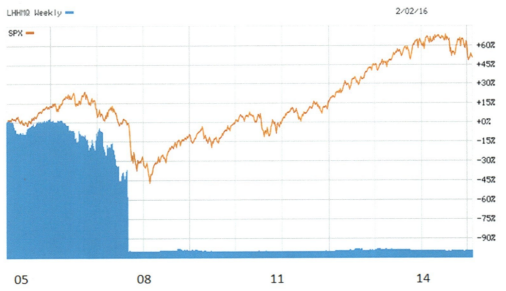

LHHMQ Weekly ▬   2/02/16

SPX ▬

Lehman Brothers Chart (LHHMQ) versus Standard and Poor's 500 Index (SPR)

Many people face problems that seem overwhelming to them. Alcoholics Anonymous (AA) is an organization that deals with such conflicts every day. They have a prayer to help their members deal with the conflict between the desire to drink and the inevitable harm it can cause for an alcoholic to do so. The AA organization uses the Serenity Prayer as part of its 12 step program, but the origins of the prayer come from German-Americans horrified by the atrocities of the Nazis during World War II. Part of that prayer includes:

"GOD, grant me the serenity to accept the things I cannot change, courage to change the things I can, and the wisdom to know the difference."

Pretty heady stuff, but it works in more ways than treatment of alcohol addiction. It gives you three options for dealing with a conflict situation – 1) accept it, 2) fix it, or 3) leave it. It really isn't any more complicated than that, yet it couldn't be harder to do in some situations.

Sometimes you can stand up to the sources of a conflict situation and change the scenario. It takes courage and talent to do this effectively. It is not easy telling the boss that he/she is not only wrong, but wrong in a big way. Not a career enhancing path in many organizations. The fable about the emperor's new clothes comes to mind. It took an innocent child who had no fear of retribution to say what everyone else already knew. The emperor was naked.

Many "grown-ups" in that story of the emperor's new clothes chose option 1. They weren't willing to fix the problem, so they chose to live with it and pretend the emperor's new clothes were simply splendid. Of course, most people would attribute this action to a lack of courage, but that would be unfair to those who would risk life and limb just to point out the emperor was being swindled by his tailors. Certainly, option 1 is considered less "honorable" than option 2, but as Goldsmith noted long ago, "He who fights and runs away, May live to fight another day; But he who is battle slain, Can never rise to fight again." So, it may be wise to pick your battles judiciously.

Everyone has a different tolerance level so I will not pass judgment on those who choose acceptance over confrontation in certain situations. When presented with this hypothetical situation some time ago, I was asked when I would speak up about the emperor's new clothes. I remember responding that the emperor could be a nasty, vengeful sort who could ruin my life, but his nakedness had little impact on me, so I would probably not confront him and his tailors. But, if his henchmen came around insisting that everyone else get naked so the emperor wouldn't notice his own lack of clothing, then I would speak up at that point.

The last option to a conflict is to refuse to participate and leave the situation. Sometimes you can't change the conflict and you can't accept it either. The only honorable choice at that point is to disengage from the activity. This tends to be a really difficult decision for many people because they either feel like a failure, a coward, or both. However, if one is truly unable to affect the situation and cannot tolerate it, then what other choice exists?

Well, there is another choice but it is not a good one for the individual or the organization. That choice is to stick around and bitch about it. It is much easier to do, makes you feel like your objection is being heard, and absolves you of responsibility for the consequences. However, this is truly the coward's way. We have all done it to some degree or another, but it is a poisonous position that affects the individual as well as the organization. Every organization has someone like this and everyone knows who it is. Don't be that person. Try to find a way to fix the problem. Try to live with those things you cannot control or influence. And when neither of those work, try to find a suitable exit. Anything else is failure.

One more thought about responding to conflict. You can tell quickly if your leadership is failing in your organization. When people get frustrated with rules, limitations, challenges and other day-to-day hardships, they often find a confrontational means of dealing with the problem. It is basically the "lose-lose" scenario. It is the "if I am going down, I'm taking you with me" approach to problem resolution.

Everyone knows an opossum will try to run from a human if it can, but when cornered it can be a fierce beast. Humans often have another means of acting out. I call it "malicious compliance". You might hear it called "work to the rule" or "doing exactly as you are asked" or "passive aggression" or some other variant.

In any case, it is a sure fire way to know there is a leadership problem that needs resolution. Malicious compliance can produce some short term benefits, but usually just makes everyone mad and hurts everyone in the long run. If it is happening to you, then you need to assess your leadership and make some changes pronto or risk losing your standing.

Let me provide an example. The situation has been slightly modified from the actual case to make the example more universal, but I suspect it is an experience that has been seen in many forms.

Leadership Lesson – Malicious Compliance

A manufacturing facility had been running at breakneck speed for some time and as a result some maintenance had been delayed to keep up the production schedule. Over time, management became accustomed to both the increased output and the lower maintenance costs, so the process continued. Eventually, habitability in the plant went from OK, to bad, to occasionally dangerous. The staff operating the plant became discontented and some suffered injury due to the deteriorating conditions. As morale fell and production needs ramped up, mistakes began to occur. Many mistakes were due to failure to follow established procedures, so management instituted a "zero tolerance" or "verbatim compliance" policy with respect to procedures.

At this point the crew had enough. So, during the next start up cycle of the plant they encountered an error in the procedures. There were four pumps (A, B, C, and D) that needed to be vented before putting them into operation. However, the procedure specified the directions for venting the A pump, but at the end of the steps simply said, "Repeat steps 1 through 13". It did not specify which pump to repeat the steps on. So, the duly chastised and frustrated crew continued to vent the A pump for the entire shift because the verbatim procedure did not specify venting any other pumps. This meant that the production for that shift was lost and the plant was nowhere closer to getting on line than it was at the beginning of the shift.

Of course, everyone in the crew knew what the procedure was intended to do, but being under strict orders to use "verbatim compliance", they were faced with a choice. They had no authority to change the procedure on the fly. They were faced with severe penalties for not following procedures verbatim. So, they accepted the situation as it was and they kept venting the A pump.

When lower management ordered the crew to vent the other pumps and proceed with startup, the crew cited the "verbatim compliance" policy and the "zero tolerance" policy for failing to follow the procedures as the reason they could not proceed. So, the management realized they were in a bind. They had created the discontent by ignoring the needs of the crew for safety and pushing them for more production. They had also instituted a "zero tolerance" policy which left them with no room to apply reasonable judgment. The crew refused to deviate from the management policies until the policies were formally changed which meant certain high level managers had to meet, issue a new policy, conduct training on the new policy, etc. Eventually, the management agreed to fix the maintenance issues affecting crew safety and abolish the "verbatim compliance" policy. Amazingly (or perhaps not so amazingly) production ramped back up and the process moved on.

So, in the short term, the "malicious compliance" strategy succeeded in getting the maintenance done and production resumed. However, there was a period of lack of production that was permanently lost and the lasting impact of the action was to breed mistrust between the management and the crew. When the ability to confer to solve problems disappears from your organization, malicious compliance will emerge and some serious soul searching and fence mending will be required to recover from it.

Dealing with Conflict

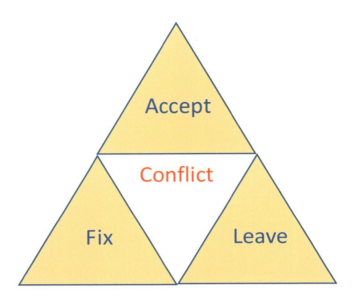

Probability Theory

At this point I wish to insert just a few elements of probability theory into our discussion about leadership. It may seem odd at first, but really isn't all that strange once you think about it a little bit. We would all like to believe that the universe is a causal landscape where certain actions result in certain consequences. However, it is not always easy to know, account for and control all the potential actions that can affect an outcome. Thus, the resulting outcome can be different despite all of our efforts to control the variables that are part of the process.

The simplest example is flipping a coin. No matter how we try, a fair coin flipped any one time may come up heads or tails (ignoring the very low probability that it lands and comes to rest on its edge). It may come up heads many times in a row. Or not. Probability theory is the mathematical means of making sense of occurrences for which we are unable to predict in advance the outcome. Such processes are said to involve "uncertainty" and this can be expressed in a mathematical form that allows us to reasonably project future behavior based on a knowledge of the possible outcomes and their relative probabilities.

In probabilistic risk assessment the process involves laying out a scenario of possible consequences arising from an event and assessing the likelihood of various combinations of successes and failures to determine the most likely ways that a desirable or an undesirable outcome can occur. However, since each step along the way is governed by probability and associated uncertainty, there is no guarantee that for any given initiating event occurrence that a particular outcome will be guaranteed to occur. In this case, there is a term for optimizing the chances of reaching a desirable outcome. In mathematics this is called "maximizing the utility function". In layman's terms, it is choosing the paths that have the better probability of having a desirable outcome than an undesirable outcome. Sounds simple, right? However, any probabilistic risk assessor will also tell you that you can take all the correct actions and have an undesired outcome. You can also take few correct actions and have positive outcome. Each are governed by the laws of probability, which just like the flip of a coin may come up heads or tails. The probabilities will be different but they do not guarantee one outcome or the other. Or as some wise man once said, "No amount of planning replaces dumb luck."

There are some implications of probability theory for leaders that cannot be ignored. Among them are what I call the Leadership Rules of Probability listed below.

1. Anything that can happen eventually WILL happen if given sufficient opportunities to occur.
2. Leaders cannot change Rule #1.
3. Leaders can influence the scenarios (the Kobiashi Maru Effect)

The only known way to "prevent something from happening" is to make it physically impossible to occur. For a satirical example, one could prevent automobile deaths by simply abolishing automobiles. Of course, deaths would still occur due to other means of transportation, just not via automobiles. So, if something bad can occur, it will eventually occur unless you can change the scenario (to the "null set" as mathematicians would say). Generally, the absurdity of a leader achieving such a change is beyond reason, which is why the second rule exists.

But there is a third option. This is the option that extraordinary leaders reach for.

Leadership Lesson – The No Win Scenario

If you are familiar with the Star Trek movies, there is a test given to students at Star Fleet Academy where they simulate being in command of a star ship when a distress call from the ship "Kobiashi Maru" comes in. They indicate that their propulsion is disabled and they are drifting into the Neutral Zone which separates Federation space from Romulan space. Entry of a warship by either party violates the truce between the two super powers and can result in an intergalactic war. So, the Federation ship commander is faced with a dilemma. Enter the neutral zone to save the Kobiashi Maru and risk intergalactic war, or leave the crew to die as the ship loses power to support life on board. The computer simulation is set up to cause the Kobiashi Maru crew to die if the Federation does not attempt the rescue and it is set up to have a host of Romulan war ships destroy both the Kobiashi Maru and the Federation ship if it enters the Neutral Zone.

Naturally, in this intentionally no-win scenario, whichever choice the student makes ends in disaster. This leaves some students puzzled and angry because it does not measure their abilities to lead. They are then informed that it is not a test of their tactical capabilities but a test of their character. Some accept the idea and others have a more difficult time with the concept. Of course, there is one student who successfully rescues the Kobiashi Maru, destroys the Romulan threat, and returns safely to home base. That would be Captain James T. Kirk, whose response is that he does not believe in the no-win scenario. So, he reprograms the scenario to allow him a fighting chance to win.

The point is that there comes a time when changing the scenario (thinking outside the box) is the only option for avoiding disaster. Operations "en extremis" has widely been accepted as justification for throwing out the rules and doing "what is necessary" to achieve the greater good. It is an ongoing dilemma regarding the ends justifying the means that has been with us since the beginning of time, but leaders need to understand when they are entering the "en extremis" scenario in order to act accordingly.

Another example of the first Leadership Rules of Probability comes from the story of the three envelopes. A well respected leader is being fired due to a problem that occurred in his organization. His replacement feels bad about his leaving and asks if he has any advice for him. The outgoing leader says, "Yes, I have prepared three envelopes for you to guide you through the inevitable crises you will face. Each card in the envelopes has three words on it. They are in the third drawer of your desk. You should only open them in order as the crises arise and do exactly as they direct. Good luck!"

The new leader is a bit shocked but has plenty of work to do to deal with his new responsibilities, so he goes about his business. In due course, things are not progressing well and he is called in to discuss the poor performance of his group with his boss. So, he opens envelope #1 and the card inside has three words on it.

BLAME YOUR PREDECESSOR

Having no better defense, the new leader goes in and tells his boss that the problems were left over from his predecessor and he needs some time to get things straightened out and he knows what needs to be done. Off the hook for the time being.

Sometime later, another meeting with the boss was scheduled to deal with the less than stellar improvements that had been achieved. So, the new leader opens the second envelope and reads the three words on the card.

REORGANIZE YOUR UNIT

The new leader goes to his boss with his reorganization plan and how he can improve productivity with an organization better aligned to the company's goals. Off the hook for the second time.

But, as things typically do, the first Leadership Rule of Probability becomes manifest and trouble rears its ugly head again. The distraught leader reaches into his drawer and nearly faints when he sees the three words on the card in the third envelope.

PREPARE THREE ENVELOPES

Thus, rule #1 stipulates that it is only a matter of time between occurrences of trouble and only by changing the scenario (rule #3) can the leader avoid the consequences of the failure. Of course, moving on to a new position before having to prepare three envelopes is a time proven means of avoiding career ending situations, but it takes great talent (or a bit of luck) to pull that maneuver off. Sooner or later the leader will be faced with that test of character presented by the Kobiashi Maru.

Leadership Versus Authority

Most times when people talk about leadership, they do so in the context of an organizational structure such as a company business, a military unit, a church hierarchy, or a sports team. It is a common assumption that leadership is an attribute expected of individuals in positions of authority in organizations. But, is leadership truly a function of organizational structure? Reality indicates otherwise, as there are myriad examples of organizational positions where minimal leadership is practiced as well as examples of leadership outside of an organizational unit. For example, few people would classify their experience going to their department of motor vehicles for a license or to renew/change plates for their car as an experience filled by inspirational leadership. And, when a traffic accident occurs and several strangers act together to pull someone from a burning vehicle, certainly the reason is not due to the presence of some organizational structure. There is a difference between leadership to influence the actions of others and wielding of authority to influence the actions of others.

Authority is the designation of individuals to make decisions on behalf of others. Organizations identify positons and matching authority to go along with each position. Those in a "position of authority" are expected to make decisions that affect the organization for the benefit of its objectives and goals. Leadership, on the other hand, is a means of interacting with people (in an organization or not) to achieve a common goal or mission. So, it is related to authority and effects the outcome from the exercise of authority, but is not authority itself.

There is a difference between power and persuasion. In simplest terms, power is the ability to impact the actions of another without their consent. Persuasion is getting others to act for a common goal based on their consent. If I demand that you show up for work promptly at eight o'clock Monday through Friday or you will lose your job, that demand is an exercise of raw power. Do as I say or suffer the consequences. It is not leadership. If, on the other hand, as a coach of a basketball team, I indicate that we need to practice every day next week for three hours a day to prepare for the conference championship tournament and everyone on the team understands that this is needed to achieve the common goal of winning the championship, then this is not a demand. This is communication of a necessary element of achieving the goal. This is leadership.

In the United States in particular, and Western Civilization in general, the concept of willing surrender of some individual sovereignty to an organization for the collective good is a fundamental cornerstone of our society. Thus, individuals willingly join organizations such as the military or a company to achieve mutually beneficial goals (protecting the country or providing for a family's welfare). In doing so, there is a tacit agreement to cede authority to members of that organization to make some decisions that will affect the sovereignty of the individual in exchange for the benefit of being a member of that organization. Thus, we elect to trade some freedom and sovereignty for security of some kind by doing so.

Nevertheless, obedience to authority is not without limits. There are degrees of subservience that are a function of the nature of the command given. Generally, the more serious the consequences of the command, the less leeway is appropriate in deciding to obey or not. Sometimes a little tyranny is a good thing.

Leadership Lesson – Power versus Leadership

One of the most dangerous evolutions undertaken in a submarine is rising from the depths of the oceans to go to periscope depth where visual contact can be made with the surrounding world. Most ships of the world occupy the surface of the oceans and some feet below that as their realm of existence. Thus, as a submarine approaches that area of operation, it is like merging from a long, open country road onto a crowded highway. The merge must be carefully made to avoid potential catastrophe. During the transition between the relative safety of deep water to the more congested surface spaces, a submarine is most vulnerable. Everyone in the control room is busy doing their individual jobs to bring the submarine safely to the desired depth, but it is the officer of the deck (OOD) who has the primary responsibility for doing so and is authorized to issue commands to the crew during the evolution.

No one speaks except as necessary to complete the task at hand. There is no frivolity, everyone is serious. You can feel the tension in the air. One command, more than any other, is understood by all to require immediate and unquestioned obedience and compliance: Emergency Deep! Whenever uttered by the OOD, everyone in the control room immediately and without further orders takes action to increase depth as rapidly as possible to avoid a collision with a surface ship or other threat to the submarine. This is command and obedience, not leadership.

However, not every order from an OOD demands the same level of immediate execution. For example, if a submarine has an operating limit of 800 feet due to hull integrity issues and the OOD on routine transit orders depth increased to 1000 feet, I promise you that someone will question the order before executing it. This is a just and appropriate action as the crew gives the OOD a chance to correct what appears to be an obvious error. This is not blind obedience. This is subordinates giving a senior an opportunity to avoid a dangerous situation. This is an example of leadership operating upward in an organization rather than downward.

What Is The Opposite Of Love?

As Tina Turner sang many years ago in a hit song, "What's love got to do, got to do with it? What's love but a second hand emotion?" Good question. The answer – EVERYTHING. I am going to fall back on some mathematical principles to make a point here, so bear with me.

Mathematicians and engineers always start a problem with a definition of some theorem, formula, or principle. So, let's begin there. Math is basically about two things, sets and functions (or maps). (OK, so I deviate from the number three sometimes. Sue me.) Sets are collections of things (usually numbers in math) and functions are rules for operating on members of the sets to produce other members of the set. OK, but you are still wondering what does love to do with leadership?

Suppose we define love in a similar way to a function in math. That is, love is a deeply felt emotion that compels action for the benefit of others. Think about that for a second. We are not talking about sex, marriage, familial identity, or other of the more common areas where the term "love" might come up. We are talking about a fundamental structure that has three parts. It is a deeply felt EMOTION. It COMPELS action. It benefits OTHERS.

Back to grade school math, let's take the set of integers and the functions of addition and multiplication. In particular, let's take the integers 2 and 3. If I add 2 and 3, I get 5. If I multiply them I get 6. So both addition and multiplication are functions operating on integers that produce other integers. Obviously, they are different functions because they produce a different result.

Now, if you ask most people what the opposite of love is, the immediate gut reaction will be that the opposite of love is hate. If we define hate as a deeply felt emotion that compels action to the detriment of others, that would be true.

But let's take a look at what being the opposite means in mathematical logic. In that case, it is not the result that defines the opposite (or inverse). It is the nature of the function that defines whether a function is the inverse of the other. Thus, hate and love are both deeply felt emotions compelling action toward others. Logically, they are not opposite functions. You cannot use the fact that the results are different or you would have to conclude that multiplication is the opposite of addition because the answer is 6 for multiplication and 5 for addition. Does anyone think the opposite of addition is multiplication? More likely you think subtraction is the opposite of addition. In fact, multiplication is just a shorthand way of describing repetitive addition.

Now this leaves us with a problem. We still do not have a definition of the opposite of love. Hmmmmmm. So, let's think. What is the opposite of a deeply felt emotion that compels action toward others? Could it be an emotion which prevents action or compels inaction and indifference toward others? What would we call such a condition? I'll give you a hint, it is a word that starts with the letter D. Cue Jeopardy theme music here.

That's right, DESPAIR! Despair is the opposite of love and you have all experienced it at one time or another. Despair makes you feel like nothing you can do will matter. Like nothing worthwhile can be achieved. Like nothing is worth trying. Like nothing matters. When you are in despair, you neither love nor hate. You cannot bring yourself to act either toward the benefit or detriment of others. It is the ultimate shutdown button on your soul.

But have you thought about it in terms of leadership? We discussed earlier that courage was overcoming fear to take actions to benefit others. How do you do that in when you are in despair? We talked about using talent to get things done and talked about being honest and understanding your situation in the world (updating your map). Despair shuts down courage and fear. Despair erases your map and prevents you from using your talent. In despair, there are no unmet expectations because expectations don't matter. In despair, there are no conflicts of conscience because your soul is shutdown.

But love is the opposite of despair. As long as there is a spark of love alive, there is hope and there is the possibility of overcoming despair. Everyone who thinks about love and despair being opposites and understanding WHY they are opposites will have an "AHA" moment. That moment when something that has been gnawing away in your subconscious suddenly emerges into your conscious mind and explodes into your understanding. Now you can look back on the failures and successes of your life and see how love and despair affected you.

Leadership Lesson – Driving Out Despair

As a leader, your job is to first drive despair out of your life. You have to do it consciously and continuously because it is ever present and ever detrimental to your well-being. Get up each day and drive despair out of your life to the extent that you can. Replace it with love and watch your accomplishments soar.

Then drive despair out of your organization or sphere of influence. Despite hard times, injustices, and any other condition that is horrible to your organization, find a way to drive despair out of the lives of those you seek to lead. Leadership fails when despair is allowed to flourish. Leadership succeeds when despair is banished to the greatest extent possible. DRIVE DESPAIR OUT! And you will be a successful leader.

What Do Leaders Do?

OK, so you want to be a leader and you have an understanding of the Foundational Principles along with the activities involving Unmet Expectations and Conflicts. You feel compelled to act in a way that benefits those you seek to lead. Now what? What is the structure or system that allows you to put those concepts into practice? I have another example and it comes in the form of a word which is an eponymous acronym: AID. Your job is to AID and that word has three parts to it.

A is for ASSIST. Your job is to assist those you are leading to accomplish a common goal. For the most part this involves the "What" and "How" items needed to avoid unmet expectations. Getting everyone on the same page (or at least a portion of their maps that are common and shared) is the "What" part. Making sure they have the training, skill, practice, tools, and time to accomplish the mission is the How part. It sounds easy until you realize that it is rare that you will actually have all of these items perfectly aligned. So, you make lemonade if all you have are lemons. But you make sure that those for whom you are serving are not expecting champagne.

I is for INSPIRE. As I noted before, motivation belongs to the individual. The leader must adjust the scenario and environment in order to align the individual's motivations and talents with the needs of the organization. People like to know that what they are doing is worthwhile and that they are contributing to a greater purpose than themselves alone. Providing that vision of the importance of their work to the success of the mission along with appreciation for their efforts in accomplishing that mission are integral to inspiring people to perform well. This is where balance between the successes and failures comes in. Celebrating success and working to overcome failure gives people hope and helps drive despair out of your organization.

D is for DEPEND. Everyone wants to feel that what they do is important. Furthermore, if the mission could be achieved by your work alone, what would you need followers for? The very fact that the work will be done by others is a tacit admission that the work is beyond the capability of a single individual.

Making people understand that the success of the mission depends on them provides them with ownership and a sense of responsibility for successful completion of tasks. Making that dependence known to others enhances the esteem for that individual or unit. There are fewer more powerful words a leader can utter than, "I depend on you."

This last piece has a critical component that people who want to be leaders need to comprehend and embrace. While virtually every task you undertake as a leader will require you to depend on others for its successful completion, the responsibility remains firmly planted on your shoulders. That means that both success and failure accrue to you.

It may seem odd or unfair that you get credit when there is no way you could accomplish everything on your own. Unfortunately, some "leaders" think that credit belongs solely or primarily with themselves. Go back to the discussion of honesty if you find yourself in this position and adjust your map.

Similarly, it also means that failure can occur due to actions of others that are beyond your direct control. It doesn't matter. You are still responsible. Some "leaders" try to minimize this chance by trying to exert control over as many parts of the process as possible. The term "micromanager" is often used in this context. The micromanager tries to exert control over all decisions and never delegates authority to others to do their functions.

Leadership Lesson – Delegate Authority not Responsibility

Recognizing that they cannot do everything and MUST rely on others for success of the common goal, the leader can relinquish control to succeed. The leader understands the maxim, "You can delegate authority, but you cannot delegate responsibility." Unfortunately, we live in a world where people acquire power and authority as a function of their positions in organizational structures. It is right and appropriate that those with the responsibility for tasks have the authority and means of achieving them. However, it is an unfortunate consequence that once obtained, authority is coveted and held close while attempting to delegate responsibility to others. Authority is not unlike Love. You get the most from it when you give most of it away.

Harken back for a moment to the discussion about probability theory earlier. One can take all the correct actions and still have an undesired outcome. Also, one can take few correct actions and have a desired outcome. For the leader, the HONEST understanding is that responsibility falls upon the leader in either case. If you cannot accept that responsibility for undesired outcomes that accrue to you even when that outcome is due to no error or neglect on your part, then you are not ready to be a leader.

What Leaders Do

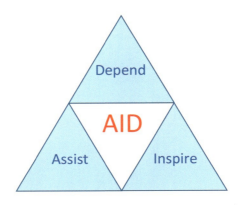

What Is Leadership?

OK, I played a trick on you. Normally, you start a conversation about a topic by trying to establish a common understanding. This usually takes the form of establishing a definition and some rules. In fact, I did just that in previous sections. But I was being devious for a reason.

"ATOYS" is an acronym for "Age and Treachery Overcomes Youth and Skill." It was the name of a co-ed softball team my wife and I belonged to some years ago. We weren't the youngest or most talented team, but we won the county softball championship nonetheless. I employed ATOYS to take you on a journey to define leadership because, quite frankly, that is how I came upon it.

I am still on the journey and probably will be all my life, but that's OK with me. I don't mind not knowing everything and don't mind making non-tragic mistakes along the way. I enjoy the journey and each new discovery along the way. I wrote this lesson in leadership in part to document my journey but more so to make your journey a little less painful, a little less frustrating, and hopefully a little more rewarding. As I mentioned earlier, I was shocked and dismayed that there was no formal, academic training on ethical leadership when I attended the Naval Academy back in the dark ages of 1970 to 1974 (that is a double entendre for those who were at the academy as the "dark ages" has a special meaning to a Mid).

So what is leadership? **<u>Leadership is no more, no less, than taking actions to influence others for their benefit in a cause greater than themselves alone.</u>** It has nothing to do with power and authority, but has everything to do with how power and authority should be wielded.

There is a subtle yet important distinction in that definition. It is about making others successful in a cause greater than themselves. That implies that the cause is just and elevates the participants to a greater good. Therefore, influencing people to commit crimes against others a la Stalin, Hitler, Pol Pot, and a host of other nefarious sorts is not leadership, it is evil. Hitler wasn't a leader, he was a despicable merchant of death and despair. So too the others on that list.

So, the choice is yours. Do you want to influence others to their benefit? Do you want to drive despair out of your life and out of the lives of others? Do you want to make others successful? CONGRATULATIONS! You are on the journey of a leader. A journey that never ends, is never complete, cannot be perfectly attained, but is worthy of all you have to give to it. So I repeat the words that appeared earlier in this text.

"And the world will be better for this.
That one man scorned and covered with scars,
Still strove with his last ounce of courage,
To reach the unreachable star."

The Power of Three

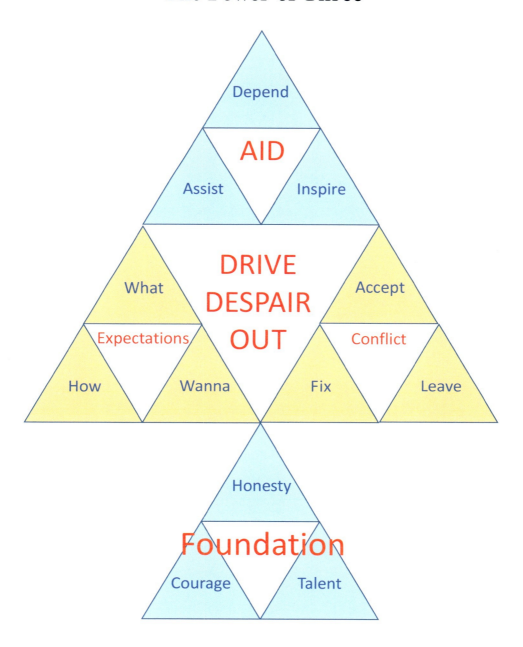

51

About The Author

Steven was born in Charleston, West Virginia into and Air Force family (both parents at one point) and is proud to be called a military brat. He traveled the country and the world following his father during his career as an Air Force Sergeant. Having spent more of that time in Texas and San Antonio in particular, he considers himself a Texan at heart even though his own career has taken him far afield. He grieves every spring when the blue bonnets are in bloom and he is not there to enjoy them.

He graduated from the United States Naval Academy on June 5, 1974 having majored in math (after a brief foray into chemistry) and was selected for the Navy Nuclear Power program in spite of one of the shortest interviews of all time with Admiral Rickover. He earned his gold dolphins aboard the USS Los Angeles (SSN-688) which was the lead ship in the Navy's fleet of attack submarines. Navy travel took him from Norfolk to the Mediterranean Sea, through the Panama Canal to Pearl Harbor and even beautiful downtown Diego Garcia among other ports of call. Being on the "First and Finest" brought with it a bevy of visits from dignitaries including the Aga Khan, assorted movie stars, and President Jimmy Carter and the First Lady.

His subsequent career involved safety and risk evaluations of nuclear power plants for the Idaho National Laboratory (INL), the civilian nuclear power industry in the United States and Canada, and government service with the Nuclear Regulatory Commission staff. He obtained a master's degree in electrical engineering via the GI Bill while working full time at the INL. Throughout this period he indulged his love for the game of golf which endures to this day and a 30 year avocation as a baseball and basketball official from which he retired to be able to watch his own children play sports.

He resides in Ashburn, Virginia in the suburbs of Washington, D.C. with his wife Barbara who has managed to put up with him for over 23 years. He has six children (including a set of triplets), five grandchildren and a 95 pound Rhodesian Ridgeback named Sunstone's Jasiri (Jazz) who likes to hog most of the space on the bed.

He is passionate about story-telling and the general subject of leadership, having to learn most of what he knows through the college of hard knocks and the grace of the sailors and shipmates he served with while they tolerated his mistakes and taught with that genteel manner that only bubbleheads understand or will elaborate on (they don't call it the silent service for nothing). Steve believes that leaders are made, not born, and that teaching others how to lead is the most rewarding and vital occupation anyone can participate in.

Steve can be reached any time at semcon@comcast.net to talk about leadership and swap sea stories. Of course, you must understand the difference between sea stories and fairy tales. Fairy tales all begin with "Once upon a time" while sea stories always begin with "This is no BS." After that, they are identical.

Printed in the United States
By Bookmasters